JULES FEIFFER

FANTAGRAPHICS BOOKS

SEATTLE, WASHINGTON

FANTAGRAPHICS BOOKS

7563 Lake City Way NE
Seattle, WA 98115 USA

Edited by Gary Groth
Covers designed by Bob Sikoryak
Interior designed by Preston White
Production assistance by Paul Baresh
Promotion by Eric Reynolds
Published by Gary Groth & Kim Thompson

First Fantagraphics Books edition: February 2003

ISBN 1-56097-501-6

Printed in Canada

FOREWORD

Jules Feiffer's *The Great Comic Book Heroes* was originally published in 1965. By that time, Feiffer had established himself as a social critic and a barbed and satiric observer of personal relationships through his strip *Feiffer* that had begun appearing in the *Village Voice* in 1956. But either because of or despite his growing status as a New York intellectual and a burgeoning playwright (*The Explainers*, 1961) and novelist (*Harry: The Rat with Women*, 1963), it was suggested to him by an editor at Dial Press (New York) that he write a book about the subject that had captivated him in his youth and influenced his career choice: comic books. He agreed to do so and the result was *The Great Comic Book Heroes*. (The editor was an aspiring novelist by the name of E.L. Doctorow.)

This is probably the first sustained essay on comic books of the '40s and '50s. Nowadays, it is practically a de rigueur subject of University dissertations, but in 1965 no one wrote about comic books, much less superhero comics. Today, our budding academicians subject superheroes to Lacanian psychoanalysis and Derridaean philosophical speculation. Thankfully, Feiffer knew better than to apply ponderous theoretical models to the superhero comics he enjoyed in his youth; in their absence, he delivers a fond reminiscence of what it was like to have thrilled to the new four-color medium as a kid from the point of view of a literate adult – intellectually playful, never condescending, qualities that are no longer deemed sufficiently serious for the study of old superhero comics. And when he theorizes, when he describes the anti-social virtues of junk, for instance, it's eminently rooted in human experience – *his* experience.

He also has the advantage of having been there at (almost) the beginning: his recollections of reading comics segue seamlessly into his earliest recollection of working in the comics business in 1945.

The original edition appeared in hardcover and contained 127 pages of the comics Feiffer talked about – stories starring Superman, Wonder Woman, Captain America, and so forth. In our streamlined 2003 edition, we felt that the comics were no longer needed; in our more enlightened times, Marvel and DC Comics are providing reprints of most of those comics in handsome hardcover editions that are readily available to anyone interested in reading them. Thus, this edition is in an affordable trade paperback format.

We are proud to put this classic back in print where it belongs.

– Gary Groth
Seattle, December 30, 2002

I have known many adults who have treasured throughout their lives some of the books they read as children. I have never come across any adult or adolescent who had outgrown comic-book reading who would ever dream of keeping any of these "books" for any sentimental or other reason.

FREDRIC WERTHAM,
SEDUCTION OF THE INNOCENT

"What th-?"

SUPERMAN, *ACTION COMICS*

1.

INTRODUCTION

Comic books, World War II, the Depression, and I all got going at roughly the same time. I was eight. *Detective Comics* was on the stands, Hitler was in Spain, and the middle class (by whose employment record we gauge depressions) was, after short gains, again out of work. I mention these items in tandem, not only to give color to the period, but as a sly historic survey to those in our own time who, of the items cited, only know of comic books.

Eight was a bad age for me. Only a year earlier I had won a gold medal in the John Wanamaker Art Contest for a crayon drawing on oak tag paper of Tom Mix jailing an outlaw. So at seven I was a winner — and didn't know how to handle it. Not that triumph isn't at any age hard to handle, but the younger you are the more of a shock it is to learn that it simply doesn't change anything. Grownups still wielded all the power, still could not be talked back to, still were always right however many times they contradicted themselves. By eight I had become a politician of the

1

grownup, indexing his mysterious ways and hiding underground my lust for getting even until I was old enough, big enough, and important enough to make a bid for it. That bid was to come by way of a career. (I knew I'd never grow big enough to beat up everybody; my hope was to, somehow, get to own everything and fire everybody.) The career I chose, the only one that seemed to fit the skills I was then sure of — a mild reading ability mixed with a mild drawing ability — was comics.

So I came to the field with more serious intent than my opiate-minded contemporaries. While they, in those pre-super days, were eating up *Cosmo, Phantom of Disguise; Speed Saunders;* and *Bart Regan, Spy,* I was counting how many frames there were to a page, how many pages there were to a story — learning how to form, for my own use, phrases like: ∂X4#?/; marking for future reference which comic book hero was swiped from which radio hero: Buck Marshall from Tom Mix; the Crimson Avenger from the Green Hornet ...

There were, at the time, striking similarities between radio and comic books. The heroes were the same (often with the same names: Don Winslow, Mandrake, Tom Mix); the villains were the same: Oriental spies, primordial monsters, cattle rustlers — but the experience was different. As an apprentice pro I found comic books the more tangible outlet for fantasy. One could put something down on paper — hard-lined panels and balloons, done the way the big boys did it. Far more satisfying than the radio serial game: that of making up programs at night in bed, getting the voices right, the footsteps and door slams right, the rumbling organ background right — and doing it all in soft enough undertones so as to escape being caught by that grownup reading Lanny Budd in the next room who at any moment might give his spirit-shattering cry: *"For the last time stop talking to yourself and go to sleep!"* Radio was too damn public.

My interest in comics began on the most sophisticated of levels, the daily newspaper strip, and thereafter

proceeded downhill. My father used to come home after work, when there was work, with two papers: the *New York Times* (a total loss) and the *World-Telegram*. The *Telegram* had *Joe Jinks* (later called *Dynamite Dunn*), *Our Boarding House*, *Out Our Way*, *Little Mary Mixup*, *Alley Oop* — and my favorite at the time, *Wash Tubbs*, whose soldier of fortune hero, Captain Easy, set a standard whose high point in one field was Pat Ryan and, in another, any role Clark Gable ever played.

For a while the *Telegram* ran an anemic four-page color supplement that came out on Saturdays — an embarrassing day for color supplements. They so obviously belonged to Sunday. So except for the loss of Captain Easy, I felt no real grief when my father abandoned the *Telegram* to follow his hero, Heywood Broun, to the *New York Evening Post*. The *Post* had *Dixie Dugan*, *The Bungle Family*, *Dinky Dinkerton*, *Secret Agent 6 ⅞*, *Nancy* (then called *Fritzi-Ritz*), and that master-piece of sentimental naturalism, *Abbie an' Slats*. I studied that strip — its Sturges-like characters, its Saroyanesque plots, its uniquely cadenced dialogue. No strip other than Will Eisner's *Spirit* rivaled it in structure. No strip, except Milton Caniff's *Terry*, rivaled it in atmosphere.

There were, of course, good strips, *very* good ones in those papers that my father did not let into the house. The Hearst papers. The *Daily News*. Cartoons from the outlawed press were not to be seen on weekdays, but on Sundays one casually dropped in on Hearst-oriented homes (never very

Nancy © 1938
United
Feature
Syndicate

3

clean, as I remember) and read *Puck, The Comic Weekly*, skipping quickly over *Bringing Up Father* to pounce succulently on page two: *Jungle Jim* and *Flash Gordon*. Too beautiful to be believed. When *Prince Valiant* began a few years later, I burned with the temptation of the damned: I begged my father to sell out to Hearst. He never did. My Hearst friends and I drifted apart. My cause lost its urgency; my attention switched to *Terry and the Pirates* — in the *Daily News* — more hated in my house than even Hearst. Why, I must have wondered in kind, was it my lot to be a Capulet when the best strips were Montagues?

It should have been a relief, then, when the first regularly scheduled comic book came out. It was called *Famous Funnies* and, in sixty-four pages of color, minutely

Terry and the Pirates © 1935 Chicago Tribune-N.Y. News Syndicate, Inc.

reprinted many of my favorites in the enemy camp. Instead, my reaction was that of a movie purist when first confronted with sound: this was not the way it was done. Greatness in order to remain great must stay true to its form. This new form, so jumbled together, so erratically edited and badly colored, was demeaning to that art — basic black and white and four panels across — that I was determined to make my life's work. I read them, yes I read them: *Famous Funnies* first, then *Popular Comics*, then *King*— but with always a sense of being cheated. I was not getting top performance for my dime.

Not until March, 1937, when the first issue of *Detective Comics* came out. Original material had previously been used in comic books, but almost all of it was in the shape and style of then existing newspaper strips.* *Detective Comics* was the first of the originals to be devoted to a single theme — crime fighting. And it looked different. Crime was fought in larger panels, fewer to a page. Most stories were complete in that issue (no more of the accursed "to be continued ...") And a lot less shilly-shallying before getting down to the action. A strange new world: unfamiliar heroes, unfamiliar drawing styles (if style is the word) — and written (if written is the word) in a language not very different from that of a primer:

> In every large city there are G-Men. In every large seaport there are G-Men known as Harbor Police. 'Speed' Cyril Saunders is a special operative in a unit of the river patrol.

So began story one, issue one of *Detective Comics*.

The typical comic book circa 1937-38 measured about 7 ¼ by 10 ¼, averaged sixty-four pages in length, was glisteningly processed in four colors on the cover and flatly and indifferently colored on the inside, if colored at all. (For in the early days some stories were still in black and white; others in tones of sickly red on one page, sickly blue on another, so that it was quite possible for a character to have a white face and blue clothing for the first two pages of a story and a pink face and red clothing for the rest.) They didn't have the class of the daily strips but, to me, this enhanced their value. The daily strips, by their sleek professionalism, held an aloof quality which comic books,

---

The Funnies in 1929; *Detective Dan* in 1933; *New Fun* in 1935. The single unique stroke in the pre *Detective Comics* days was the creation, by Sheldon Mayer, of the humor strip, *Scribbly* — an underrated, often brilliantly wild cartoon about a boy cartoonist with whom, needless to say, I identified like mad. 1 regret that it is not within the province of this book to give Mayer or *Scribbly* the space both of them deserve.

being not quite professional, easily avoided. They were closer to home, more comfortable to live with, less like grownups.

The heroes were mostly detectives of one kind or another; or soldiers of fortune; here and there, even a magician. Whatever they were, they were tall, but not too tall — space limitations, you see; they were dark (blond heroes were an exception, possibly because most movie heroes were dark, possibly because it was a chance for the artist to stick in a blob of black and call it hair. The blond heroes, in every case, were curly-haired. The dark heroes, when full color came in, turned blue); they were handsome — well, symbolically handsome. The world of comics was a form of visual shorthand, so that the average hero need not have been handsome in fact, so long as his face was held to the required arrangement of lines that readers had been taught to be the accepted sign of handsome: sharp, slanting eyebrows, thick at the ends, thinning out toward the nose, of which in three-quarter view there was hardly any — just a small V placed slightly above the mouth, casting the faintest nick of a shadow. One never saw a nose full view. There was never a full view. They were too hard to draw. Eyes were usually ball-less, two thin slits. Mouths were always thick, quick single lines — never double. Mouths, for some reason, were rarely shown open. Dialogue, theoretically, was spoken from the nose. Heroes' faces were square-jawed; in some cases, all-jawed. Often there was a cleft in the chin. Most heroes, whatever magazine they came from, looked like members of one of two families: Pat Ryan's or Flash Gordon's. Except for the magicians, all of whom looked like Mandrake. The three mythic archetypes.

That first *Detective Comics*, aside from its groundbreaking role, is memorable for the debut of Creig Flessel, not then a good illustrator, but within the first half-dozen issues to become one of the best in the business — a master of the suspense cover. And another debut: that of Jerry Siegel and Joe Shuster, then in their *pre-Superman*

days, weighing in with a slam-bang, hell-for-leather cross between Victor McLaglen and Captain Easy (with a Flash Gordon jaw), appropriately named *Slam Bradley*, because slamming was what he did most of the time. Always, of course, against bad guys — and always having a wonderful time. It was this action-filled rawness, this world of lusty hoodlumism, of Saturday movie serials seven days a week that made the new comic books, from their first day of publication, the principal reading matter in my life. That, plus the pragmatic insight that here, in a field where they hardly knew how to draw at all, I could make my earliest gains.

I studied styles. There was Tom Hickey, who lettered with disconcerting open W's (**W**); who used an awful lot of dialogue ("printing" was the hated word for it in my neighborhood) to tell a painfully slow-moving story, full of heroes named Ian. Too thin-blooded. Too English.

There was Will Ely, a Caniff gone wrong, whose Pat Ryanish heroes lay flat on the paper, the shadows on their clothing more imposing than they were. The villains were

WITH MOCK GRAVITY VAL EXCLAIMS:— *"HERE, WHERE I STAND, LONG AGO STOOD CAESAR. CAESAR MADE HIS DECISION, CROSSED THE RUBICON AND TOOK ROME. WHEN ROMAN ENVOYS DEMANDED TRIBUTE OF KING ARTHUR, HE UNCEREMONIOUSLY HUSTLED THEM OUT OF ENGLAND. AS ENGLISH KNIGHTS, WE MAY NOT BE SO POPULAR IN ROME!"*

Prince Valiant © 1940 King Features Syndicate

usually bald with a few MacArthurish strands of hair —
burly butcher boys smelling of sweat. In a fair fight they
could easily take the hero — and often did, the first couple
of times. Never in the end. But by that time I no longer
cared. If the bad guy won every fight save the last, I had
my doubts.

There was Fred Guardineer, whose career was
magicians — he drew more than anybody, all of them
looking like Mandrake. Top hat, tails, flossy tie, mustache,
glassy eyes. Each magician was equipped with an enormous
brown servant not named Lothar. Guardineer's magicians,
whatever they were called, wherever they were published,
cast their spells by speaking backwards. "SKCOR KAERB
NWOD LLAW!" Zatara would cry and rocks, rising from
nowhere, would break down that wall. A fine point: could
anybody speaking backwards have Zatara's magic — a
villain for instance? The metaphysics shaky, the drawing
style stiff, I gave up on Fred Guardineer.

The problem in pre-super days was that, with few
exceptions, heroes were not very interesting. And, by any
realistic appraisal, certainly no match for the villains who
were bigger, stronger, smarter (as who wasn't?), and even
worse, were notorious scene stealers. Who cared about
Speed Saunders, Larry Steele, Bruce Nelson, et al., when
there were Oriental villains around? Tong warriors
lurking in shadows, with trident beards, pointy
fingernails, and skin the color of ripe lemons. With
narrow, missile-like eyes slantingly aimed at the nose; a
nose aged and curdled with corrupt wisdom, shriveled in
high expectancy of the coming tortures on the next page.
How they toyed with those drab ofay heroes: trap set, trap
sprung, into the pit, up comes the water, down comes the
pendulum, out from the side come the walls. Through an
unconvincing mixture of dumb luck and general science,
the hero escaped, just barely; caught and beat up the
villain: that wizened ancient who, in toe-to-toe combat,
was, of course, no match for the younger man. And
readers were supposed to cheer? Hardly! The following

month it all happened again. Same hero, different Oriental, slight variance in the torture.

Villains, whatever fate befell them in the obligatory last panel, were infinitely better equipped than those silly, hapless heroes. Not only comics, but life taught us that. Those of us raised in ghetto neighborhoods were being asked to believe that crime didn't pay? Tell that to the butcher! Nice guys finished last; landlords, first. Villains by their simple appointment to the role were miles ahead. It was not to be believed that any ordinary human could combat them. More was required. Someone with a call. When *Superman* at last appeared, he brought with him the deep satisfaction of all underground truths: Our reaction was less "How original!" than "But, of course!"

Leaping over skyscrapers, running faster than an express train, springing great distances and heights, lifting and smashing tremendous weights, possessing an impenetrable skin — these are the amazing attributes which Superman, savior of the helpless and oppressed, avails himself of as he battles the forces of evil and injustice.

SUPERMAN, *ACTION COMICS*, AUGUST 1939

2.

The advent of the superhero was a bizarre comeuppance for the American dream. Horatio Alger could no longer make it on his own. He needed "Shazam!" Here was fantasy with a cynically realistic base: Once the odds were appraised honestly, it was apparent you had to be super to get on in this world.

The particular brilliance of Superman lay not only in the fact that he was the first of the superheroes,* but in the concept of his alter ego. What made Superman different from the legion of imitators to follow was not that when he took off his clothes he could beat up everybody — they all did that. What made Superman extraordinary was his point of origin: Clark Kent.

Remember, Kent was not Superman's true identity as Bruce Wayne was the Batman's or (on radio) Lamont Cranston the Shadow's. Just the opposite. Clark Kent was the fiction. Previous heroes — the Shadow, the Green Hornet, The Lone Ranger — were not only more vulnerable;

*Action Comics, June 1938

they were fakes. I don't mean to criticize; it's just a statement of fact. The Shadow had to cloud men's minds to be in business. The Green Hornet had to go through the fetishist fol-de-rol of donning costume, floppy hat, black mask, gas gun, menacing automobile, and insect sound effects before he was even ready to go out in the street. The Lone Ranger needed an accoutremental white horse, an Indian, and an establishing cry of Hi-Yo Silver to separate him from all those other masked men running around the West in days of yesteryear.

But Superman had only to wake up in the morning to be Superman. In his case, Clark Kent was the put-on. That fellow with the eyeglasses and the acne and the walk girls laughed at wasn't real, didn't exist, was a sacrificial disguise, an act of discreet martyrdom. *Had they but known!*

And for what purpose? Did Superman become Clark Kent in order to lead a normal life, have friends, be known as a nice guy, meet girls? Hardly. There's too much of the hair shirt in the role, too much devotion to the imprimatur of impotence — an insight, perhaps, into the fantasy life of the Man of Steel. Superman as a secret masochist? Field for study there. For if it was otherwise, if the point, the only point, was to lead a "normal life," why not a more typical

Superman #1
© 1939-1940
DC Comics

identity? How can one be a cowardly star reporter, subject to fainting spells in time of crisis, and not expect to raise serious questions?

The truth may be that Kent existed not for the purposes of the story but for the reader. He is Superman's opinion of the rest of us, a pointed caricature of what we, the noncriminal element, were really like. His fake identity was our real one. That's why we loved him so. For if that wasn't really us, if there were no Clark Kents, only lots of glasses and cheap suits which, when removed, revealed all of us in our true identities — what a hell of an improved world it would have been!

Superman #I © 1939-40 DC Comics

In drawing style, both in figure and costume, Superman was a simplified parody of Flash Gordon. But if Alex Raymond was the Dior for Superman, Joe Shuster set the fashion from then on. Everybody else's super-costumes were copies from his shop. Shuster represented the best of old-style comic-book drawing. His work was direct, unprettied — crude and vigorous; as easy to read as a diagram. No creamy lines, no glossy illustrative effects, no touch of that bloodless prefabrication that passes for professionalism these days. Slickness, thank God, was

Superman #3 © 1939-1940 **DC Comics**

beyond his means. He could not draw well, but he drew single-mindedly — no one could ghost that style. It was the man. When assistants began "improving" the appearance of the strip it promptly went downhill. It looked as though it were being drawn in a bank.

But, oh, those early drawings! Superman running up the sides of dams, leaping over anything that stood in his way (No one drew skyscrapers like Shuster. Impressionistic shafts, Superman poised over them, his leaping leg tucked under his ass, his landing leg tautly pointed earthward), cleaning and jerking two-ton get-away cars and pounding them into the sides of cliffs — and all this done lightly, unportentously, still with that early Slam Bradley exuberance. What matter that the stories quickly lost interest; that once you've made a man super you've plotted him out of believable conflicts; that *even* super-villains, super-mad scientists and, yes, super-Orientals were dull and lifeless next to the overwhelming image of that which Clark Kent became when he took off his clothes. So what if the stories were boring, the villains blah? This was the Superman Show— a touring road company backing up a great star. Everything was a stage wait until he came on. Then it was all worthwhile.

Besides, for the alert reader there were other fields of interest. It seems that among Lois Lane, Clark Kent, and Superman there existed a schizoid and chaste *menage à trois*. Clark Kent loved but felt abashed with Lois Lane;

Superman saved Lois Lane when she was in trouble, found her a pest the rest of the time. Since Superman and Clark Kent were the same person this behavior demands explanation. It can't be that Kent wanted Lois to respect him for himself, since himself was Superman. Then, it appears, he wanted Lois to respect him for his fake self, to love him when he acted the coward, to be there when he pretended he needed her. She never was — so, of course, he loved her. A typical American romance. Superman never needed her, never needed anybody — in any event, Lois chased *him* — so, of course, he didn't love her. He had contempt for her. Another typical American romance.

Love is really the pursuit of a desired object, not pursuit by it. Once you've caught the object there is no longer any reason to love it, to have it hanging around. There must be other desirable objects out there, somewhere. So Clark Kent

Superman #4 © 1939-1940 DC Comics

acted as the control for Superman. What Kent wanted was just that which Superman didn't want to be bothered with. Kent wanted Lois, Superman didn't — thus marking the difference between a sissy and a man. A sissy wanted girls who scorned him; a man scorned girls who wanted him. Our cultural opposite of the man who didn't make out with women has never been the man who did — but rather the man who could if he wanted to, but still didn't. The ideal of masculine strength, whether Gary Cooper's, Li'l Abner's, or Superman's, was for one to be so virile and handsome, to be in such a position of strength, that he need never go near girls. Except to help them. And then get the hell out. Real rapport was not for women. It was for villains. That's why they got hit so hard.

The Shield — symbol of Americanism and all America stands for — truth, justice, patriotism, courage. The Shield is no importation from another planet nor an accidental freak of nature. He is the product of years of painstaking toil, the climax to brilliant scientific research.

THE SHIELD, *SHIELD-WIZARD COMICS,*
WINTER ISSUE, 1940

3.

The problem with other superheroes was that the most convenient way of becoming one had already been taken. Superman was from another planet. One of the self-denigrating laws of all science fiction is that *every* other planet is better than ours. Other planets may have funny-looking people but they think better, know more languages (including English), and are much further along in the business of rocketry and destruction. So, by definition, Superman had to be super: No outer-space weakling had *ever* been let in. The immediate and enormous success of Superman called for the creation of a tribe of successors — but where were they to come from? Not from other planets; Superman had all other planets tied up legally. Those one or two superheroes who defied the ban were taken apart by lawyers (nothing is as super as a writ).

The answer, then, rested with science. That strange bubbly world of test tubes and gobbledy-gook which had, in the past, done such great work in bringing the dead back to life in the form of monsters — why couldn't it also

make men super? Thus Joe Higgins went into his laboratory and came out as the Shield; and John Sterling went into his laboratory and came out as Steel Sterling; and Steve Rogers went into the laboratory of kindly Professor Reinstein and came out as Captain America; and kindly Professor Horton went into his laboratory and came out with a synthetic man, named, illogically, the Human Torch. Science had run amok!

And not only science. With business booming comic-book titles, too, ran amok: *Whiz, Startling, Astonishing, Top Notch, Blue Ribbon, Zip, Silver Streak, Mystery Men, Wonder World, Mystic, Military, National, Police, Big Shot, Marvel-Mystery, Jackpot, Target, Pep, Champion, Master, Daredevil, Star-Spangled, All-American, All-Star, All-Flash, Sensation, Blue Bolt, Crash, Smash,* and *Hit Comics.* Setting loose a menagerie of flying men, webbed men, robot men, ghost men, minuscule men, flexible-sized men — men of all shapes and costume blackening the comic-book skies like locusts in drag.

Skyman, Sky Chief, The Face, The Sub Mariner, The Angel, The Comet, The Hangman, Mr. Justice, Uncle Sam, The Web, The Doll Man, Plastic Man, The White Streak — all scrambling for a piece of the market. Their magazines

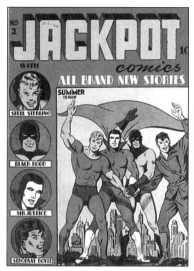
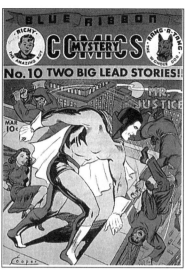

were competitively dated months ahead, so that if *Big Shot* released an issue in January and dated it March, in reprisal *All-American* would date its February issue August. Aficionados began to check: comic books not dated a minimum of four months in advance were deemed shabby. One was hesitant to be seen with them.

Understandably, this Pandora's box of men-of-steel was viewed gravely by Superman. One story of the time, denied by everyone, but for years a legend in the business and reported as such, was that rival impresarios, worried lest the Superman people bring legal or marketing reprisals (their distributive arm circulated not only their own, but most other comic books), volunteered certain major concessions. Such as capes. It was granted that Superman, being the *premier danseur* of superheroes, was the only one entitled to wear a cape. All others were, with appropriate ceremony, circumcised. (One could imagine the scene: The Shield, G-Man Extraordinary, standing in a field, his modest emblem, the American Flag, plucked from his burly shoulders, folded in half, then in quarters — neatly — so that no part touched the ground. Buried in Arlington, a choked-up marine playing taps; J. Edgar Hoover, a prominent character in the strip, standing alongside. Rumor had it

that he sent flowers.)

The most savage reprisals in comic books were, just as in revolutions, saved not for one's enemies but for one's own kind. If, for a moment, Superman may be described as the Lenin of superheroes, Captain Marvel must be his Trotsky. Ideologically of the same bent, who could have predicted that within months the two would be at each other's throats — or that, in time, Captain Marvel would present the only serious threat to the power of the man without whom he could not have existed?

From the beginning, Captain Marvel possessed certain advantages in the struggle. In terms of reader identification, Superman was far too puritanical: if you didn't come from his planet you couldn't ever be super — that was that. But the more liberal Captain Marvel left the door open. His method of becoming super was the simplest of all — no solar systems or test tubes involved — all that was needed was a magic word: "Shazam!"

"Pie in the sky!" retorted the pro-Superman bloc, but millions of readers wondered. If all it took was a magic word, then all that was required was the finding of it. Small surprise that for a while Captain Marvel caught and

passed the austere patriarch of the super-movement.

More than that, Captain Marvel was gifted with the light touch. Billy Batson, the newsboy, who Captain Marvel truly was, was drawn by artist C. C. Beck as an oval-faced, dot-eyed, squiggly-haired boy familiar to any child who ever sent for a how-to-draw-heads course. The magic for readers in Captain Marvel was that not only did it appear easy to become him, it looked easy to draw him. Deceptively so. Captain Marvel was better drawn, really, than Superman. C. C. Beck followed in the tradition of Roy Crane's *Wash Tubbs,* drawing with a virginal simplicity that at times was almost sticklike — but still there was style. Villains ranged from mad scientist Dr. Sivana (the best in the business), who uncannily resembled Donald Duck, to Mr. Mind, a worm who talked and wore glasses, to Tawky Tawny, a tiger who talked and wore a business suit. A Disneyland of happy violence. The Captain himself came out dumber than the average superhero — or perhaps less was expected of him. A friendly fullback of a fellow with apple cheeks and dimples, he could be imagined being a buddy rather than a hero, an overgrown boy who chased villains as if they were squirrels. A perfect fantasy figure for, say, Charlie Brown. His future seemed assured. What a

shock, then, the day Superman took him to court.

Happily, I did not learn of the Superman versus Captain Marvel lawsuit until years later. It would have done me no good to discover two of my idols, staunch believers in direct action, bent over, hands cupped to lips, whispering in the ears of their lawyers. No one should have to grow up that fast.

The Superman people said that Captain Marvel was a direct steal. The Captain Marvel people said what do you mean; sheer coincidence; isn't there room for the small businessman; we don't know what you're talking about. It went on that way for years, but the outcome was clear from the start. Captain Marvel fought hard but he was a paper tiger. One wondered whether he was beginning to drink. He was losing his lean, Fred MacMurray look, fleshing out fast in the face, in the gut, in the hips, moving onward and outward to Jack Oakie.

Then too there was great disappointment in the word "Shazam!" As it turned out it didn't work for readers. Other magic words were tried. They didn't work either. There are just so many magic words until one feels he's been made a fool of. How easy it became to hate "Shazam! Shazam! Shazam!" That taunting cry that worked fine for Captain Marvel but didn't do a damn thing for the rest of us.

I had the vague feeling that Captain Marvel was making fun of me. More and more his adventures took on

Police Comics #2,
September 1941
"Plastic Man" ©
1941 DC Comics

Whiz Comics #9, © 1040 DC Comics, Inc.

the tone of parodies — item: Billy Batson being turned into a baby by mad scientist Dr. Sivana and thus not being able to say the magic word, it coming out "Tha-Tham!" I was not prepared for frivolousness on the part of my superheroes! When the *Captain Marvel* people finally settled the case and went out of business, I couldn't have cared less.

Whiz Comics #12, © 1041 DC Comics, Inc.

The 'Bat-man,' a mysterious and adventurous figure fighting for righteousness and apprehending the wrongdoer, in his lone battle against the evil forces of society ... his identity remains unknown.

EPISODE ONE OF BATMAN,
DETECTIVE COMICS, MAY, 1939

4.

B atman trailed Superman by a year and was obviously intended as an offshoot, but his lineage — the school of rich idlers who put on masks — dates back to the Scarlet Pimpernel and includes Zorro, and The Green Hornet, with whom Batman bears the closest as well as most contemporaneous resemblance. Both the Green Hornet and Batman were wealthy, both dabbled in chemistry, both had super-vehicles, and both costumed themselves with a view toward striking terror into the hearts of evildoers. The Green Hornet buzzed; the Batman flapped — that was the essential difference.

Not that there weren't innovations: Batman popularized in comic books the strange idea, first used by the Phantom in newspapers, that when you put on your mask, your eyes disappeared. Two white slits showed — that was all. If that didn't strike terror into the hearts of evildoers, nothing would.

Batman, apparently, was in better physical shape than the Green Hornet, less dependent on the creature comforts

of super-vehicles, or the rich man's use of nonlethal gas warfare. Batman got more meaningfully into the fray and, in consequence, was more clobbered. Though a good deal was made of his extraordinary stamina much of it, as it turns out, was for punishment — another innovation for superheroes: There was some reason to believe he had a glass jaw.

But Batman was not a superhero in its truest sense (however we may have liked to think of him). If you pricked him, he bled — buckets. Superman's superiority lay in the offense, Batman's lay in the rebound. Whatever was done to him, whatever trap laid, wound opened, skull fractured, all he had to show for it was a discreet patch of Band-aid on his right shoulder. With Superman we won; with Batman we held our own. Individual preferences were based on the ambitions and arrogance of one's fantasies.

The Batman school preferred a vulnerable hero to an invulnerable one, preferred a hero who was able to take punishment and triumph in the end to a hero who took comparatively little punishment, just dished it out. I suspect the Batman school of having healthier egos. In my own case, the concept of triumph over adversity was never very

Batman #1, Spring 1940 © 1940 DC Comics

Batman #1, Spring 1940
© 1940 DC Comics

convincing. My own observations led me to believe that the only triumph most people eked out of adversity was to manage to stay alive as it swept by. With me, I didn't think it would be any different. I preferred to play it safe and be Superman.

Another point: I couldn't have been Batman even if I wanted to. If I were *ever* to be trapped in a steel vault with the walls closing in on all sides, I was obviously going to have to break out with my fists because it was clear from my earliest school grades that I was never going to have the know-how to invent an explosive in my underground laboratory that would blow me to safety. I was lousy at science. And I found the thought of having an underground laboratory chilling. My idea of a superhero was some guy, bad with his hands, who came from an advanced planet so that he didn't have to go to the gym to be strong or go to school to be smart. The sort of superhero I admired had to be primarily passive, but invulnerable.

What made Batman interesting, then, was not his strength but his storyline. Batman, as a feature, was infinitely better plotted, better villained, and better looking than Superman. Batman inhabited a world where no one, no matter the time of day, cast anything but long shadows — seen from weird perspectives. Batman's world was scary; Superman's, never. Bob Kane, Batman's creator, combined *Terry and the Pirates*-style drawing with *Dick Tracy*-style villains, e.g., The Joker, The Penguin, The Cat Woman, The

Batman #2,
Summer 1940
© 1940 DC
Comics

Scarecrow, The Riddler, Clay-Face, Two-Face, Dr. Death, Hugo Strange.

Kane's early drawings, pretentious and stiff, coordinated perfectly with his early writing technique — a form of florid pre-literacy so typical of comic books of that day (as witnessed in the excerpt introducing this chapter. Or another example from a Kane feature of that time:

> Africa — the dark continent whose jungles teem with insects, beasts, fever, and wild natives. A

land of terrible secrets no man can read ... up
the river to the shore of Kenya, Clip Carson,
vagabond adventurer, paddles his canoe.*)

Despite it all, I remember Clip Carson warmly — and
who, having once noted Batman smart-assing his way
through a fist fight, has not forever been taken with him?
Kane's strength, as did Shuster's, lay not in his
draftsmanship (which was never quite believable), but in
his total involvement in what he was doing (which made
everything believable). However badly drawn and crudely
written, Batman's world took control of the reader. If Kane
said so, men *did* pose stroking their chins whenever they
weren't fighting, running, or shooting in such a way that
hand and chin never quite made contact; if Kane said so,
gangsters *did* wear those peculiarly styled hats and suits —
bought off the rack from a line nobody in the world had
ever seen before; if Kane said so heads were not egg
shaped, but rectangular; chins occupied not the bottom
sixth of a face but the bottom half — because Kane's was an
authentic fantasy, a genuine vision, so that however one
might nit-pick the components, the end product remained
an impregnable whole: gripping and original. Kane, more

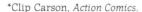

*Clip Carson, *Action Comics*.

Batman #3,
Fall 1940
© 1940 DC
Comics

than any other comic-book man (except Will Eisner, who will be discussed later), set and made believable the terms offered to the reader.

Batman's world was more cinematic than Superman's. Kane was one of the early experimenters with angle shots and though he was not as compulsively avant-garde in his use of the worm's eye, the bird's eye, the shot through the wineglass, as others in the field he was the only one of the *Detective, Adventure, Action Comics* line who managed to get that Warner Brothers fog-infested look.

For just as the movie studios had their individual trademarks, their way of lighting, their special approach to subject matter by which they could be identified even if one came in at the middle, so did comic books. National, who

Batman #4, Winter 1941
© 1941 DC Comics

produced the D.C. line, was the MGM of the field. It had
the great stars, the crisp-brittle lighting, the elder
statesman touch — smoothly exciting, eschewing the more
boisterous effects of its less wealthy competitors.
Superman was the best, but the most humorless of the
superheroes (befitting his position); Batman was the best,
but the most wooden of the masked heroes (a bit of early
Robert Taylor there) — neither was quite touchable. They
were State Department White Papers of the mind. And
National, who issued them, was the government in power.

The opposite extreme was Fox — the Monogram Studios
of the industry. Fox had the best covers and the worst
insides. The covers were rendered in a modified pulp style:
well-drawn, exotically muscled, half-undressed heroes
rescuing well-drawn, exotically muscled, half-undressed
maidens. The settings, often as not, were in the conventional
Oriental/mad scientist's laboratory — hissing test tubes
going off everywhere; a hulking multi-racial lab assistant at
the ready to violate the girl; the masked hero crashing
through a skylight, guns, aimed at nobody, flaming in each
hand; the girl, strapped to an operating table, screaming
fetchingly — not yet aware that the crisis was passed.

Since the covers of Fox books were drawn by good men
and the insides drawn by bad men, the hero on the cover
could only be connected to his facsimile on the inside by
the design of his leotards. Fox, like Monogram, had few
stars and a deeply felt plot shortage. It pushed hard on the
Green Mask, a slender, inadequate-looking hero who beat
up slender, inadequate-looking criminals. While this
business of fighting crime within one's weight division had
something to recommend it, The Green Mask, somehow,
never caught on.

To recoup, Fox made a star of the Blue Beetle, another
Green Hornet derivative (in this case, a cop in real life),
who, in order to fight criminals outside the reach of the
law, liked to dress as a beetle, this being his idea of a
symbol that would strike terror into the hearts of evildoers
(not the first cop to work outside the law, but one of the

Sheena, Queen of the Jungle.

few who had the decency to take off his uniform while doing it). As it turned out — and unpredictably — evil-doers were impressed with the Blue Beetle. His sign — the shadow of a great beetle projected into the evildoer's line of vision — struck terror into their hearts. He wore a Phantom-type uniform, with scales — rather unpleasant looking without being impressive. He was a great favorite for a far longer time than he deserved.

Fox titles included *Mystery Men Comics, Wonder World Comics, Science Comics, Fantastic Comics* — all of them washed out, never looking quite alive or quite finished — existing in a mechanical limbo. The good men working for Fox soon moved elsewhere. Fiction House, a better outfit by inches, was often the place. As Republic was to Monogram, Fiction House was to Fox. Its one lasting contribution: *Sheena, Queen of the Jungle,* signed by W. Morgan Thomas (a pseudonym), drawn and very likely written by S. R. Powell, who was later to do the best of the magician strips (not excepting Mandrake): Mr. Mystic.

Sheena was a voluptuous Tarzan who laid waste to wild beasts, savages, and evil white men in the jungle of her day, always assisted by her boyfriend, Bob, a neat, young fellow in boots and jodhpurs who mainly stayed free of harm's way while Sheena, manfully, cleaned out the trouble spots. Not as unfair a division of labor as you might think once

you saw the two of them back to back, for while the boyfriend was supposed to be taller and more muscular, it was Sheena who gave the impression of size. Standing proud in the foreground, challenging an overmatched lion to hand-to-hand combat while her admiring young man stood in the tree shadows holding her spear.

Sheena was the star of *Jungle Comics*, a book I looked at only when there was nothing but novels to read around the house. Beating up lions did not particularly interest me; my problem was with people. Nor did the people Sheena laid out interest me very much: They were the usual crop of white hunters in search of the elephants' graveyard, a strip of land so devout in its implications to jungle-book fanciers that one could only assume the elephants took instruction in the church before dying.

Fiction House books had a boxed, constipated look. Balloons were rectangular, restricted-looking. Anybody knew — or should have known — that good balloons were scalloped bubbles floating light as air on the tops of panels. Free and imaginative. Rectangular balloons were depressants — something architectural-looking about them; something textbooky. They were no more to be trusted than those cartoons that gave up balloons entirely and ran an open narrative across the bottom of the panels — cartoons trying their damnedest not to look or sound like cartoons — set in the past tense, full of he saids and she saids. The past tense was a violation of comic-book decorum (and newspaper strips too). Comics were too immediate an experience to subjugate the reader to a past tense. Written narratives posed a deliberate similarity to *real books*: those wordy enclosures that threatened knowledge, threatened advance, threatened a hold on one's soul so that one could not keep it to mark time with, but must move ahead, learn, grow — all dubious outside values. (*Prince Valiant* too was guilty of that bookish style but it was set in King Arthur's day. So l learned to live with it. But I couldn't put up with it in *Tarzan* and I could barely tolerate it in *Flash Gordon*. And I didn't like it anywhere else.)

For many criminals who managed to operate beyond the long reach of the law, the Spirit was a dead end. Still there is none of them ... er ... alive, that is ... who knows that this outlaw is really Denny Colt, a young criminologist presumed dead by the public but who continues to assist society behind the mask of the Spirit. "That he operates out of Wildwood Cemetery, where he is supposed to be buried, is known only to Commissioner Dolan and his daughter, Ellen ..."

WILL EISNER, *THE SPIRIT*, DECEMBER 1945

5.

Fiction House put out *Fight Comics, Planet Comics, Wing Comics;* its one attempt at innovation was an outsized black-and-white book called *Jumbo Comic — an* unworkable hybrid of conventional comic-book material and conventional newspaper material. Its single feature of interest was *Hawk of the Seas,* signed by Willis Rensie (Eisner spelled backwards). Hawk was a pirate feature, notable only as a trial run for *The Spirit,* full of the baroque angle shots that Eisner introduced to the business. Eisner had come to my attention a few years earlier doing a one-shot black-and-white feature called *'Muss 'Em Up' Donovan* in a comic book with the flop-oriented title of *Centaur Funny Pages.* 'Muss 'Em Up' Donovan was a detective, fired from the force on charges of police brutality (his victims, evidently, were white). Donovan is called back to action by a city administrator overly harassed by crime who feel it is time for an approach that circumvents the legalistic niceties of due process. Such administrations were in vogue in all comic books of the thirties and forties. The heroes

they culled out of the darkness operated, masked or not, outside the reach of the law. Their job: to catch criminals operating outside the reach of the law. In theory, one would think a difficult identity problem — but as it turned out in practice, not really.

Heroes and readers jointly conspired to believe that the police were honest, but inept, well-meaning, but dumb — except for good cops like Donovan, who were vicious. Arraignment was for sissies; a he-man wanted gore. Operating within the reach of the law a hero could get

WELL, WELL! IF IT ISN'T TINKER GORDON.. WHEN DID YOU GET OUT?

The Spirit (August 11, 1940) © 2000 Will Eisner

busted for that. So heroes, with the oblique consent of the power structure ("If you get into trouble, we can't vouch for you"), wandered outside the reach of the law, pummeled everyone in sight, killed a slew of people — and brought honor back to Central City, back to Metropolis, back to Gotham.

'Muss 'Em Up' Donovan was one such vigilante, a hawk-nosed, trench-coated primitive, bitter over his expulsion from office, but avid to answer the bell when

duty once again called. Pages of violence: 'Muss 'Em Up' beating the truth out of a progression of sniveling stoolies; 'Muss 'Em Up' kicking in doors; 'Muss 'Em Up' shooting and getting shot at — a one-man guerrilla war on crime. A grateful citizenry responded with vigor. 'Muss 'Em Up' was reinstated — allowed to 'Muss 'Em Up' in uniform once again. In those pre-civil-rights days, we thought of that as a happy ending.

Will Eisner was an early master of the German expressionist approach in comic books — the Fritz Lang school. *'Muss 'Em Up'* was full of dark shadows, creepy angle shots, graphic close-ups of violence and terror. Eisner's world seemed more real than the world of other comic book men because it looked that much more like a movie. The underground terror of RKO prison pictures, of convicts rioting, of armored-car robberies, of Paul Muni or Henry Fonda not being allowed to go straight. The further films dug into the black fantasies of a depression generation the more they were labeled realism. Eisner retooled this mythic realism to his own uses: black fantasies on paper. Just as with the movies, it was labeled realism.

The Spirit (August 11, 1940) © 2000 Will Eisner

Eisner's line had weight. Clothing sat on his characters heavily; when they bent an arm, deep folds sprang into action everywhere. When one Eisner character slugged another, a real fist hit real flesh. Violence was no externalized plot exercise; it was the gut of his style. Massive and indigestible, it curdled, lava-like, from the page.

Eisner moved on from Fiction House to land, finally, with the Quality Comic Group — the Warner Brothers of the business — creating the tone for their entire line: *The Doll Man, Black Hawk, Uncle Sam, The Black Condor, The Ray, Espionage — starring Black-X — Eisner* creations all. He'd draw a few episodes and abandon the characters — bequeath them to Lou Fine, Reed Crandall, others. No matter. The Quality books bore his look, his layout, his way of telling a story. For Eisner did just about all of his own writing — a rarity in comic-book men. His stories carried the same weight as his line, involving a reader, setting the terms, making the most unlikely of plot twists credible.

His high point was *The Spirit,* a comic-book section created as a Sunday supplement for newspapers. It began in 1939 and ran, weekly, until 1942, when Eisner went into

The Spirit (August 25, 1940) © 2000 Will Eisner

The Spirit **(November 24, 1940) © 2000 Will Eisner**

the army and had to surrender the strip to (the joke is unavoidable) a ghost.

Sartorially the Spirit was miles apart from other masked heroes. He didn't wear tights, just a baggy blue business suit, a wide-brimmed blue hat that needed blocking, and, for a disguise, a matching blue eye mask, drawn as if it were a skin graft. For some reason, he rarely wore socks — or if he did they were flesh-colored. I often wondered about that.

Just as Milton Caniff's characters were identifiable by their perennial WASPish, upper middle-class look, so were Eisner's identifiable by that look of just having got off the boat. The Spirit reeked of lower middle-class: his nose may have turned up, but we all knew he was Jewish.

What's more, he had a sense of humor. Very few comic-book characters did. Superman was strait-laced; Batman wisecracked, but was basically rigid; Captain Marvel had a touch of Li'l Abner, but that was parody, not humor. Alone among mystery men the Spirit operated (for comic books) in a relatively mature world in which one took stands somewhat more complex than hitting or not

The Spirit (December 1, 1940) © 2000 Will Eisner

hitting people. Violent it was — this was to remain Eisner's stock in trade — but the Spirit's violence often turned in on itself, proved nothing, became, simply, an existential exercise; part of somebody else's game. The Spirit could even suffer defeat in the end: be outfoxed by a woman foe — stand there, his tongue making a dent in his cheek — charming in his boyish, Dennis O'Keefe way — a comment on the ultimate ineffectuality of even superheroes. But, of course, once a hero turns that vulnerable he loses interest to both author and readers. The Spirit, through the years, became a figurehead, the chairman of the board, presiding over eight pages of other people's stories. An inessential do-gooder, doing a walk-on on page 8, to tie up loose strings. A masked Mary Worth.

Not that he wasn't virile. Much of the Spirit's charm lay in his response to intense physical punishment. Hoodlums could slug him, shoot him, bend pipes over his head. The Spirit merely stuck his tongue in his cheek and beat the crap out of them — a more rational response than Batman's, for all his preening. For Batman had to take off his rich idler's street clothes, put on his Batshirt, his

Batshorts, his Battights, his Batboots; buckle on his Batbelt full of secret potions and chemical explosives; tie on his Batcape; slip on his Batmask; climb in his Batmobile and go fight the Joker, who in one punch (defensively described by the author as maniacal) would knock him silly. Not so with the Spirit. It took a mob to pin him down and no maniacal punch ever took him out of a fight. Eisner was too good a writer for that sort of nonsense.

Eventually Eisner developed story lines that are perhaps best described as documentary fables — seemingly authentic when one reads them, but impossible, after the fact. There was the one about Hitler walking around in a Willy Lomanish middle world: subways rolling, Bronx girls chattering, street bums kicking him around. His purpose in coming to America: to explain himself, to be accepted as a nice guy, to be liked. Silly when you thought of it, but for eight pages, grimly convincing.

Or the man who was a million years old — whose exploits are being read about by two young archeologists of the future who discover, in mountain ruins, the tattered

The Spirit (December 1, 1940) © 2000 Will Eisner

The Spirit **(December 15, 1940)**
© 2000 Will Eisner

remains of an old Spirit pamphlet, which details his story:
the story of the oldest man in the world, cursed to live
forever for being evil, until on the top of a mountain, in
combat with the Spirit, he plunges into the ocean and
drowns. "Ridiculous story," say these archeologists of the
future as they finish the last page; these being their final
words, for coming up behind them is that very old man,
his staff raised high to crush their skulls, to toss them over
the mountain edge into the ocean, and then to dance away,
singing.

    I collected Eisners and studied them fastidiously. And I
wasn't the only one. Alone among comic-book men, Eisner
was a cartoonist other cartoonists swiped from.

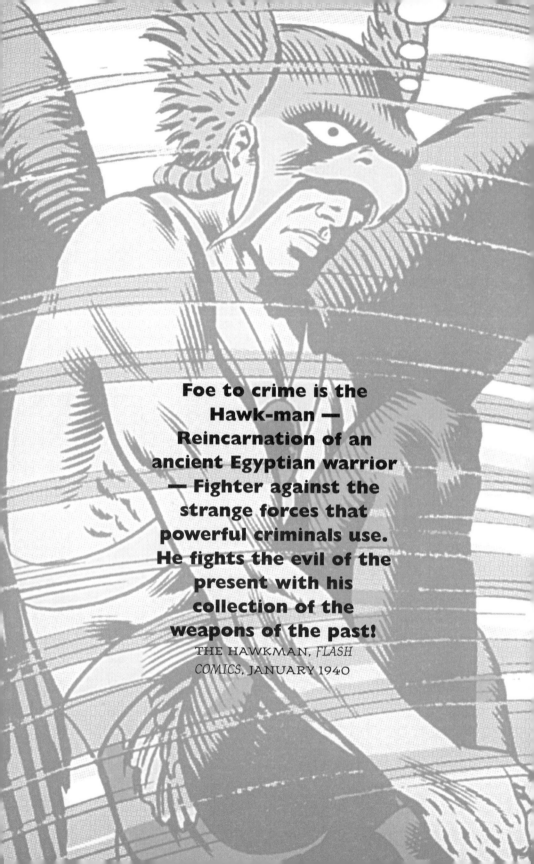

Foe to crime is the
Hawk-man —
Reincarnation of an
ancient Egyptian warrior
— Fighter against the
strange forces that
powerful criminals use.
He fights the evil of the
present with his
collection of the
weapons of the past!

THE HAWKMAN, *FLASH
COMICS*, JANUARY 1940

6.

Swiping was and is a trade term in comic books for appropriating that which is Alex Raymond's, Milton Caniff's, Hal Foster's or any one of a number of other sources and making it one's own. Good swiping is an art in itself. One can, for example, scan the first fifteen years of any National publication and catch an album of favorite *Flash Gordon* poses signed by dozens of different artists. Flash, Dale, Dr. Zarkov, and Ming the Merciless stared nakedly out at the reader, their names changed, but looking no less like themselves even if the feature did call itself *Hawkman*. Other cartoonists preferred the Caniff touch, so next to nine pages of swiped *Terry and the Pirates* there often appeared nine pages of swiped *Flash Gordon*. Then there were those who mixed their pitches — using within the same story Alex Raymond swipes, Milton Caniff swipes, Hal Foster swipes, and movie-still swipes. So that a villain might subtly shift his appearance from Raymond's Ming in one panel, to Caniff's Captain Judas in another, to Foster's Sir Modred in a third to, at last, Basil Rathbone.

Swipes, if noticed, were accepted as part of comic-book folklore. I have never heard a reader complain. Rather, I have heard swipe artists vigorously defended, one compared to another: Who did the best Caniff, the closest Raymond? *Hawkman,* a special favorite of mine, gave an aged and blended look to its swipes — a sheen so formidable, I often preferred the swipe to the original, defended the artist on economic grounds (not everybody was rich enough to hire models like those big newspaper guys), and paid his swipes the final compliment of clipping and swiping them. On occasion, swipe artists would try to be clever, try to confuse the reader by including, within a single frame, a group of figures swiped — and even changed slightly — from three or four different sources. They may have gotten away with it with others, but never me: no comic-book man could cloud the grey cells of the boy Poirot.

I not only clipped swipes, I traced and managed to get hold of their sources. I stapled them together, lay them in front of me and began my own chain of comic books. Sixty-four pages in black-and-white pencil: *Comic Caravan, Zoom Comics, Streak Comics.* Each book contained an orthodox variety of superheroes who, for their true identities, were given the orthodox assortment of prep school names: Wesley, Bruce, Jay, Gray, Oliver, Rodney, Greg, Carter — obviously the stuff out of which heroes were made — you didn't find names like that in my neighborhood. I had a

Flash Gordon
© 1934 King
Features
Syndicate

Hawkman from
All Star Comics
#12 © 1942 DC
Comics, Inc.

harder time with magicians because almost every name
was taken. There was *Mr. Mystic*, and *Merzah the Mystic*, and
Kardak the Mystic Magician, and *Nadir Master of Magic*, and
Monako Prince of Magic, and *Marvello the Monarch of
Magicians*, and *Zambini the Miracle Man*, and *Ibis the
Invincible*, and *Merlin the Magician, Yarko the Magician, Dakor
the Magician, Zanzibar the Magician, Sargon the Sorcerer*, and
Zatara.

I created a *Spirit* swipe *(The Eel)* and a *Flash* swipe *(The
Streak)*, a *Lone Ranger* swipe *(The Masked Caballero)*, a
Hawkman swipe *(The Vulture)* and even a *Clip Carson* swipe
(Gunner Dixon: "Gunner Dixon is not meant to be a bold
super athletic math genius who with his super powers
turns to do good in this war-torn world — NO! He's just an
ordinary guy, he's no mental giant, he can't lick an army
with his bare fist, but he can hold his own in any fight. All
he is, is an *American"*).

Each story was signed by a pseudonym, except for the
lead feature, which, star-conscious always, I assigned to my
real name. I practiced my signature for hours. Inside a box;
a circle; a palate. Inside a scroll that was chipped and aged,

with a dagger sticking out of it which threw a long shadow. I had a Milton Caniff-style signature; an Alex Raymond; an Eisner (years later, when I went to work for Eisner, my first assignment was the signing of his name to *The Spirit*. I was immediately better at it than he was).

To me these men were heroes. The world they lived in, as I saw it in those years of idolatry, was a world in which a person was blessedly in control of his own existence: wrote what he wanted to write, drew it the way he wanted to draw it — and was, by definition, brilliant. And thus, loved by millions. It was a logical extension of my own world — except the results were a lot better. Instead of being little and consequently ridiculed for staying in the house all day and drawing pictures, one was big, and consequently canonized for staying in the house all day and drawing pictures. Instead of having no friends because one stayed in the house all day and drew pictures, one grew up

The author's early attempt to create a superhero comic.

OUT INTO THE NIGHT RACES THE FLASH!!

I'LL GET THEM IF IT KILLS ME!!

Flash Comics #, January 1940
© 1940 DC Comics

and had millions of friends because one stayed in the house all day and drew pictures. Instead of being small and skinny with no muscles and no power because one stayed in the house all day and drew pictures, one grew up to be less small, less skinny, still perhaps with no muscles, but with lots of power: a friend of Presidents and board chairmen; an intimate of movie stars and ball players — all because one stayed in the house all day and drew pictures.

I swiped diligently from the swipers, drew sixty-four pages in two days, sometimes one day, stapled the product together, and took it out on the street where kids my age sat behind orange crates selling and trading comic books. Mine went for less because they weren't real.

To advise a child not to read a comic book works only if you can explain to him your reasons. For example a ten-year-old girl from a cultivated and literate home asked me why I thought it was harmful to read Wonder Woman (a crime comic which we have found to be one of the most harmful). She saw in her home many good books and I took that as a starting point, explaining to her what good stories and novels are. "Supposing," I told her, "you get used to eating sandwiches made with very strong seasonings, with onions and peppers and highly spiced mustard. You will lose your taste for simple bread and butter and for finer food. The same is true for reading strong comic books. If later on you want to read a good novel it may describe how a young boy and girl sit together and watch the rain falling. They talk about themselves and the pages of the book describe what their innermost little thoughts are. This is what is called literature. But you will never be able to appreciate that if in comic-book fashion you expect that at any minute someone will appear and pitch both of them out of the window." In this case the girl understood, and the advice worked.

FREDRIC WERTHAM, *SEDUCTION OF THE INNOCENT*

7.

Though I may have pirated the superheroes I never went near their boy companions. I couldn't stand boy companions. If the theory behind Robin the Boy Wonder, Roy the Superboy, The Sandman's Sandy, The Shield's Rusty, The Human Torch's Toro, The Green Arrow's Speedy was to give young readers a character with whom to identify it failed dismally in my case. The super *grownups* were the ones I identified with. They were versions of me in the future. There was still time to prepare. But Robin the Boy Wonder was my own age. One need only look at him to see he could fight better, swing from a rope better, play ball better, eat better, and live better — for while I lived in the east Bronx, Robin lived in a mansion, and while I was trying, somehow, to please my mother — and getting it all wrong — Robin was rescuing Batman and getting the gold medals. He didn't even have to live with his mother.

Robin wasn't skinny. He had the build of a middleweight, the legs of a wrestler. He was obviously an "A" student, the center of every circle, the one picked for

".. AND TONIGHT IS THE NIGHT CRAIG WORKS LATE IN THE MUSEUM! C'MON, ROBIN. LET'S RIDE!-- WE'VE GOT TO SAVE A HUMAN LIFE!"

Batman #2 © 1940 DC Comics, Inc.

greatness in the crowd — God, how I hated him. You can imagine how pleased I was when, years later, I heard he was a fag.

In *Seduction of the Innocent,* the psychiatrist Fredric Wertham writes of the relationship between Batman and Robin:

They constantly rescue each other from violent attacks by an unending number of enemies. The feeling is conveyed that we men must stick together because there are so many villainous creatures who have to be exterminated. ... Sometimes Batman ends up in bed injured and young Robin is shown sitting next to him. At home they lead an idyllic life. They are Bruce Wayne and 'Dick' Grayson. Bruce Wayne is described as a 'socialite' and the official relationship is that Dick is Bruce's ward. They live in sumptuous quarters, with beautiful flowers in large vases. ... Batman is sometimes shown in a dressing gown. ... It is like a wish dream of two homosexuals living together.

For the personal reasons previously listed I'd be delighted to think Wertham right in his conjectures (at least in Robin's case; Batman might have been duped), but conscience dictates otherwise: Batman and Robin were no more or less queer than were their youngish readers, many of whom palled around together, didn't trust girls, played games that had lots of bodily contact, and from similar

surface evidence were more or less queer. But this sort of case-building is much too restrictive. In our society it is not only homosexuals who don't like women. Almost no one does. Batman and Robin are merely a legitimate continuation of that misanthropic maleness that runs, unvaryingly, through every branch of American entertainment, high or low: literature, movies, comic books, or party jokes. The broad tone of our mass media has always been inbred, narcissistic, reactionary. Mocking Jews because most of the writers weren't; mocking Negroes because all of the writers weren't; denigrating women because all of the writers were either married or had mothers. Mass entertainment being engineered by men, it was natural that a primary target be women: who were fighting harder for their rights, evening the score, unsettling the traditional balance between the sexes. In a depression they were often able to find work where their men could not. They were clearly the enemy.

Wertham cites testimony taken from homosexuals to prove the secret kicks received from the knowledge that Batman and Robin were living together, going out together, adventuring together. But so were the Green Hornet and Kato (hmm — an Oriental ...) and the Lone Ranger and Tonto (Christ! An Indian !) — and so, for that matter, did Fred Astaire and Ginger Rogers hang around together an awful lot, but, God knows, I saw every one of their movies and it never occurred

Batman #3 © 1940 DC Comics, Inc.

Wonder Woman #1, Summer 1942 © 1942
DC Comics

to me they were sleeping with each other. If homosexual fads were certain proof of that which will turn our young queer, then we should long ago have burned not just Batman books, but all Bette Davis, Joan Crawford, and Judy Garland movies.

Wertham goes on to point to *Wonder Woman* as the lesbian counterpart to Batman: "For boys, Wonder Woman is a frightening image. For girls she is a morbid ideal. Where Batman is antifeminine, the attractive Wonder Woman and her counterparts are definitely antimasculine."

Well, I can't comment on the image girls had of Wonder Woman. I never knew they read her — or any comic book. That *girls* had a preference for my brand of literature would have been more of a frightening image to me than any number of men being beaten up by Wonder Woman.

Whether Wonder Woman was a lesbian's dream I do not know, but I know for a fact she was every Jewish boy's unfantasied picture of the world as it really was. You mean men weren't wicked and weak? You mean women weren't badly taken advantage of? You mean women didn't have to be *stronger* than men to survive in this world? Not in my house!

My problem with Wonder Woman was that I could

never get myself to believe she was that good. For if she was as strong as they said, why wasn't she tougher looking? Why wasn't she bigger? Why was she so flat-chested? And why did I always feel that, whatever her vaunted Amazon power, she wouldn't have lasted a round with Sheena, Queen of the Jungle?

No, Wonder Woman seemed like too much of a put-up job, a fixed comic strip — a product of group thinking rather than the individual inspiration that created Superman. It was obvious from the start that a bunch of men got together in a smoke-filled room and brain-stormed themselves a Super Lady. But nobody's heart was in it. It was choppily written and dully drawn. I see now that my objection is just the opposite of Wertham's: Wonder Woman wasn't dykey enough. Her violence was too immaculate, never once boiling over into a little fantasmal sadism. Had they given us a Wonder Woman with balls — that would have been something for Dr. Wertham and the rest of us to wrestle with!

Sensation Comics #10, October 1942 "Wonder Woman" © 1942 DC Comics

Rat-at-ta-tat! Rat-at-ta-tat! Hear that roll of a drum? Twee! Twee! Twee! Hear that shrill of a fife? It's a call, brother — it's a call to join the parade! You too, sister you're in on this! Get in step! Get in step! For here they come! The butcher, the baker, the girl riveter, the man machinist, the farmer, the banker, housewife, school-kid! Everybody's marching ... marching behind The Minute Man! $0 buy tho$e war bond$! Buy tho$e war $tamp$! Get in step! Get in step with Batman and Robin as they go marching on to victory with ... The Bond Wagon.

BATMAN, *DETECTIVE COMICS*, AUGUST 1943

8.

World War II was greeted by comic books with a display of public patriotism and a sigh of private relief. There is no telling what would have become of the superheroes had they not been given a *real* enemy. Domestic crime-fighting had become a bore; one could sense our muscled wonder men growing restless in their protracted beatings up of bank robbers, gang overlords, mad scientists. Domestic affairs were dead as a gut issue: Superheroes wanted a hand in foreign policy. At first this switching of fronts seemed like a progressive political step — if only by default. Pre-war conspiracies had always been fomented by the left (enigmatically described as anarchists), who put it into the minds of otherwise sanguine workers to strike vital industries in order to benefit unidentified foreign powers. Now, with the advent of war it was no longer necessary to draw villains from a stockpile of swarthy ethnic minorities: there were the butch-haircutted Nazis to contend with — looking too much like distorted mirror images of the heroes, perhaps — but

*Military Comics #12, October 1942
"Blackhawk" © 1942 DC Comics*

no less bold an innovation for the conceit that Anglo-Saxons, too, could be villains.

Consistent with the policy formalized by Chaplin's *Great Dictator*, Hitler was never portrayed as anything but a clown. All other Germans were blond, spoke their native language with a thick accent, and were very, very stupid.

Military Comics #8, March 1942 "Blackhawk" © 1942 DC Comics

Flash Gordon
© 1934 King
Features
Syndicate

The I.Q. of villains dropped markedly as the war progressed. Whatever there used to be of plot was replaced by action — great leaping gobs of it, breaking out of frames and splashing off the page. This was the golden age of violence — its two prime exponents: Joe Simon and Jack Kirby.

The team of Simon and Kirby brought anatomy back into comic books. Not that other artists didn't draw well (the level of craftsmanship had risen alarmingly since I'd begun to compete), but no one could put quite as much anatomy into a hero as Simon and Kirby. Muscles stretched magically, foreshortened shockingly. Legs were never less than four feet apart when a punch was thrown. Every panel was a population explosion — casts of thousands: all fighting, leaping, falling, crawling. Not any of Eisner's brooding violence for Simon and Kirby: that was too Liston-like. They peopled their panels with Cassius Clays — speed was the thing, rocking, uproarious speed. *Blue Bolt, The Sandman, The Newsboy Legion, The Boy Commandoes* and best of all: *Captain America and Bucky.* Like an Errol Flynn war movie. Almost always taken from secret files. Almost always preceded by the legend: "Now it can be told."

But the unwritten success story of the war was the smash comeback of the Oriental villain. He had faded badly for a few years, losing face to mad scientists — but now he was at the height of his glory. Until the war we always assumed he was Chinese. But now we knew what he was! A

Sensation Comics #8, **August 1942 "Wonder Woman" © 1942 DC Comics**

Jap; a Yellow-Belly Jap; a Jap-a-Nazi Rat: these being the
three major classifications. He was younger than his wily
forebear and far less subtle in his torture techniques (this
was war!). He often sported fanged bicuspids and drooled a
lot more than seemed necessary. (If you find the image
hard to imagine I refer you to his more recent incarnation
in magazines like Dell's *Jungle War Stories* where it turns
out he wasn't Japanese at all: He was North Vietnamese.
At the time of this book's publication the wheel will, no
doubt, have turned full circle and he'll be back to Chinese.)

The war in comic books despite its early promise, its
compulsive flag-waving, its incessant admonitions to keep
'em flying was, in the end, lost. From Superman on down,
the old heroes gave up a lot of their edge. As I was growing
up, they were growing tiresome: more garrulous than I
remembered them in the old days, a little show-offy about
their winning of the war. Superman, The Shield, Captain
America and the rest competed cattily to be photographed
with the President; to be officially thanked for selling
bonds, or catching spies, or opening up the Second Front.
The Spirit had been mutilated beyond recognition by a
small army of ghosts; Captain Marvel had become a house

joke; The Batman, shrill. Crime comics were coming in, nice art work by Charles Biro, but not my cup of tea. Too oppressive to my fantasies. Reluctantly I fished around for other reading matter, stumbled on *Studs Lonigan* — not exactly an example of Dr. Wertham's boy and girl watching the rain fall while discussing their innermost thoughts, but still it was a novel. By the age of fifteen, I had had it with comic books. I was not to read them again until I went into the business a year later.

Wash Tubbs © 1942 **NEA**

SEDUCTION OF THE INNOCENT

**Fear not, queen mother!
It was Laertes
And he shall die at my hands!
... Alas! I have been poisoned
And now I, too, go
To join my deceased father!
I, too — I-AGGGRRRAA!**

THE DEATH SCENE QUOTED BY FREDRIC
WERTHAM FROM HAMLET COMIC BOOK

Fredric Wertham, M. D.

*the influence of
comic books on today's youth*

RT

9.

Had I been only six years older I could have been in comic books from almost the beginning: carting my sample case in the spring of 1939 instead of 1945; a black cardboard folio with inside overlapping side sheets, secured tight with black bows on its three unbound corners, containing 14 x 22" pages of bristol board on which would be drawn typical adventure swipes of the day, inked with as slick a Caniff line as one could evoke at sixteen – a series of thick and thin brush strokes wafted onto the paper with the lightest, most characterless of touches. Draftsmanship was not the point here – this was technique!

Going the rounds then: checking the inside glossy covers of comic books for names and addresses, riding the subway out of the Bronx in the morning rush, my portfolio on the deck, squeezed tightly between my legs so that the crowd could not bruise it, nor art thieves steal it. The bigger houses – so official looking – would have scared me, and then dismissed me for lack ofexperience. How are you supposed to get experience when no one will give you experience? The answer: to begin low – at one of the

countless schlock houses grinding out the junk in small, brutal-looking offices all over town. These, the cheapie houses, were where one got the first breaks. Not being worth anything, no one else worth anything would hire you. But the schlock houses operated as way stations for both the beginners and the talentless.

Artists sat lumped in crowded rooms, knocking it out for the page rate. Penciling, inking, lettering in the balloons for $10 a page, sometimes less; working from yellow type scripts which on the left described the action, on the right gave the dialogue. A decaying old radio, wallpapered with dirty humor, talked race results by the hour. Half-finished coffee containers turned old and petrified. The "editor," who'd be in one office that week, another the next, working for companies that changed names as often as he changed jobs, sat at a desk or a drawing table — an always beefy man who, if he drew, did not do it well, making it that much more galling when he corrected your work and you knew he was right. His job was to check copy, check art, hand out assignments, pay the artists money when he had it, promise the artists money when he didn't. Everyone got paid if he didn't mind going back week after week. Everyone got paid if he didn't mind occasionally pleading.

The schlock houses were the art schools of the business. Working blind but furiously, working from swipes, working from the advice of others who drew better because they were in the business two weeks longer, one, suddenly, learned how to draw. It happened in spurts. Nothing for a while: not being able to catch on, not being able to foreshorten correctly, or get perspectives straight or get the blacks to look right. Then suddenly: a breakthrough. One morning you can draw forty per cent better than you could when you quit the night before. Then, again you coast. Your critical abilities improve but your talent won't. Nothing works. Despair. Then another break-through. Magically, it keeps happening. Soon it stops being magic, just becomes education.

I'd have met, in those early days, other young cartoonists. We'd talk nothing but shop. A new world; new superheroes; new arch-villains. We'd compare swipes — and then, as our work improved, we'd disdain swipes. We'd joke about those who claimed no longer to use them but, secretly, still did. Sometimes, secretly, we still did, too. Some of us would pair off, find rooms together — moving our drawing tables away from the family into the world of commercial togetherness. Eighteen hours a day of work. Sandwiches for

breakfast, lunch, and dinner. An occasional beer, but not too often. And nothing any stronger. One dare not slow up.

We were a *generation*. We thought of ourselves the way the men who began movies must have. We were out to be splendid — somehow. In the meantime we talked at our drawing tables about Caniff, Raymond, Foster. We argued over the importance of detail. Must *every* button on a suit be shown? Some argued yes. The magic realists of the business. Others argued no; what one wanted, after all, was *effect*. The expressionists of the business. Experiments in the use of angle shots were carried on. Arguments raged: Should angle shots be used for their own sake or for the sake of furthering the story? Everyone went back to study *Citizen Kane*. Rumors spread that Welles, himself, had read and learned from comic books! What a great business!

The work was relentless. Some men worked in bull pens during the day; free-lanced at night — a hard job to quit work at five-thirty, go home and free-lance till four in the morning, get up at eight and go to a job. And the weekends were the worst. A friend would call for help: He had contracted to put together a sixty-four-page package over the weekend — a new book with new titles, new heroes — to be conceived, written, drawn, and delivered to the engraver between six o'clock Friday night and eight-thirty Monday morning. The presses were reserved for nine.

Business was booming. New titles coming out by the day, too many of them drawn over a two-day weekend. Cartoonists throughout the city took their pencils, pens, brushes, and breadboards to apartments already crowded with drawing tables, fluorescent lamps, folding chairs, and crippling networks of extension cords. Writers banged out

the scripts, handed them by the page to an available artist — one who was not penciling or inking his own page, or assisting on backgrounds on someone else's. Jobs were divided and subdivided — or sometimes, not divided at all. An artist might not work from a script, but write his own story, in which case it would be planned in pencil right on the

finished page. Some artists penciled only the figures, leaving the backgrounds for another artist who then passed the page to a lettering man who then passed the page to an inker who then might ink only the figures, or sometimes only the heads, passing the work, then, to another inker who finished the bodies and the backgrounds. Everybody worked on everybody else's jobs. The artist who contracted the job would usually take the lead feature. Other features were parceled out indiscriminately. No one cared too much. No one was competitive. They were all too busy.

If the place being used had a kitchen, black coffee was made and remade. If not, coffee and sandwiches were sent for — no matter the hour. In mid-town Manhattan something always had to be open. Except on Sundays. A man could look for hours before he found an open delicatessen. The other artists sat working, starving: some dozing over their breadboards, others stretching out for a nap on the floor, their empty fingers twitching to the rhythm of the brush. During heavy snow storms stores that stayed open were hard to find. A food forager I know of returned to the loft rented for the occasion, a loft devoid of kitchen, stove, hot plate, utensils, plates or can opener, with two dozen eggs and a can of beans. Desperate with rage

and hunger and the need to get back to the job, the artists scraped tiles off the bathroom wall, built the tiles into a small oven, set fire to old scripts, heated the beans in the can (which was opened by hammering door keys into it with the edge of a T-square) and fried the eggs on the hot tiles. They used cold tiles for plates.

This was the birth of a new art form! A lot of talk about that: how to design better, draw better, animate a figure better — so that it would jump, magically, off the page. Movies on paper — the final dream!

But even before the war, the dream began to dissipate. The war finished the job. The best men went into the service. Hacks sprouted everywhere — and, with sales to armed forces booming, hack houses also sprouted, declared bankruptcy in order to not pay their bills, then re-sprouted under new names. The page rates went up to $15 a page for penciling, $10 for inking, $2 for lettering. Scripts got $5 to $7 a page — few artists wrote their own any more. Few cared.

The business stopped being thought of as a life's work and became a steppingstone. Five years in it at best, then on to better things: a daily strip, or illustrating for the *Saturday Evening Post,* or getting a job with an advertising agency. If you weren't in it for the buck, there wasn't a single other reason.

Talk was no longer about work. The men were too old, too bored for that. It was about wives, baseball, kids, broads — or about what a son of a bitch the guy you were working for was: office gas. The same as in any office anywhere, not a means of communication but a ritualistic discharge. The same release could be achieved through clowning: joke phone calls, joke run-around errands for the office patsy, joke disappearances of the new man's artwork. Everyone passed it off as good fun in order not to be marked as a bad sport. By the end of the war the men who had been in charge of our childhood fantasies had become archetypes of the grownups who made us need to have fantasies in the first place.

TEEN-AGE ROMANCES

Caught!

The Confession Of
A "Good-Time" Girl.

10¢

Respect for parents, the moral code, and for
honorable behavior, shall be fostered.

Policemen, judges, government officials and
respected institutions shall never be presented
in such a way as to create disrespect for
established authority.

In every instance good shall triumph over evil
and the criminal punished for his misdeeds.

FROM THE CODE OF THE COMICS MAGAZINE ASSOCIATION OF AMERICA

No. 14

AFTERWORD

1.

In the years since Dr. Wertham and his supporters launched their attacks, comic books have toned down considerably, almost antiseptically. Publishers in fear of their lives wrote a code, set up a review board, and volunteered themselves into censorship rather than have it imposed from the outside. Dr. Wertham scorns self-regulation as misleading. Old-time fans scorn it as having brought on the death of comic books as they once knew and loved them: for, surprisingly, there *are* old comic book fans. A small army of them. Men in their thirties and early forties wearing school ties and tweeds, teaching in universities, writing ad copy, writing for chic magazines, writing novels — who continue to be addicts, who save old comic books, buy them, trade them, and will, many of them, pay up to fifty dollars for the first issues of *Superman* or *Batman;* who publish and mail to each other mimeographed "fanzines" — strange little publications

AND SO AS THE UGLIEST MAN POISES THE DEADLY NEEDLE OVER THE HELPLESS WOMAN, SUDDENLY, A HISS, AND....

Batman #3, Fall 1940 © 1940 DC Comics

deifying what is looked back on as "the golden age of comic books." Ruined by Wertham. Ruined by growing up.

So Dr. Wertham is wrong in his contention, quoted earlier, that no one matures remembering the things.

His other charges against comic books — that they were participating factors in juvenile delinquency and, in some cases, juvenile suicide, that they inspired experiments, a la Superman, in free-fall flight which could only end badly, that they were, in general, a corrupting influence, glorifying crime and depravity — can only, in all fairness, be answered: "But of course. Why else read them?"

Comic books, first of all, are junk.* To accuse them of being what they are is to make no accusation at all: There is no such thing as *uncorrupt* junk or *moral* junk or *educational* junk — though attempts at the latter have, from time to time, been foisted on us. But education is not the purpose of junk (which is one reason why *True Comics* and *Classic Comics* and other half-hearted attempts to bring reality or literature into the field invariably looked embarrassing). Junk is there to entertain on the basest,

---

*There are a few exceptions, but nonjunk comic books don't, as a rule, last very long.

most compromised of levels. It finds the lowest fantasmal
common denominator and proceeds from there. Its choice
of tone is dependent on its choice of audience, so that
women's magazines will make a pretense at veneer scorned
by movie-fan magazines, but both are, unarguably, junk. If
not to their publishers, certainly to a good many of their
readers who, when challenged, will say defiantly: "I know
it's junk, but I like it." Which is the whole point about junk.

Green Lantern #1, Fall 1941
© 1941 **DC Comics**

It is there to be nothing else but liked. Junk is a second-
class citizen of the arts; a status of which we and it are
constantly aware. There are certain inherent privileges in
second-class citizenship. Irresponsibility is one. Not being
taken seriously is another. Junk, like the drunk at the
wedding, can get away with doing or saying anything
because, by its very appearance, it is already in disgrace. It
has no one's respect to lose; no image to endanger. Its
values are the least middle-class of all the mass media.
That's why it is needed so.

The success of the best junk lies in its ability to come
close, but not too close; to titillate without touching us. To
arouse without giving satisfaction. Junk is a tease; and in
the years when the most we need is teasing we cherish it —

The Spirit (September 8, 1940)
© 2000 Will Eisner

in later years when teasing no longer satisfies we graduate, hopefully, into better things or, haplessly, into pathetic and sometimes violent attempts to make the teasing come true.

It is this antisocial side of junk that Dr. Wertham scorns in his attack on comic books. What he dismisses— perhaps because the case was made badly — is the more positive side of junk. (The entire debate on comic books was, in my opinion, poorly handled. The attack was strident and spotty; the defense, smug and spotty — proving, perhaps, that even when grownups correctly verbalize a point about children, they manage to miss it: so that a child expert can talk about how important fantasies of aggression are for children, thereby destroying forever the value of fantasies of aggression. Once a child is told: "Go on, darling. I'm watching. Fantasize," he no longer has a reason.) Still, there is a positive side to comic books that more than makes up for their much publicized antisocial influence. That is: their *underground* antisocial influence.

2.

Adults have their defense against time: It is called "responsibility," and once one assumes it, he can form his life into a

set of routines which will account for all those hours when he is fresh, and justifies escape during all those hours when he is stale or tired. It is not size or age or childishness that separates children from adults. It is "responsibility." Adults come in all sizes, ages, and differing varieties of childishness, but as long as they have "responsibility" we recognize, often by the light gone out of their eyes, that they are what we call grownup. When grownups cope with "responsibility" for enough number of years they are retired from it. They are given, in exchange, a "leisure problem." They sit around with their "leisure problem" and try to figure out what to do with it. Sometimes they go crazy. Sometimes they get other jobs. Sometimes it gets too much for them and they die. They have been handed an undetermined future of nonresponsible time and they don't know what to do about it.

And that is precisely the way it is with children. Time is the ever-present factor in their lives. It passes slowly or fast, always against their best interests: Good time is over in a minute; bad time takes forever. Short on "responsibility," they are confronted with a "leisure problem." That infamous question: "What am I going to do with myself?" correctly rephrased should read: "What am I going to do to get away from myself?"

Wonder Woman #1, Summer 1942 © 1942 DC Comics

And then, dear God, there's school! Nobody really knows why he's going to school. Even if one likes it, it is still, in the best light, an authoritarian restriction of freedom where one has to obey and be subservient to people not even his parents. Where one has to learn, concurrently, book rules and social rules, few of which are taught in a way to broaden horizons. So books become enemies and society becomes a hostile force that one had best put off encountering until the last moment possible.

Police Comics #15,
January 1943
"Plastic Man"
© 1943 **DC Comics**

Children, hungry for reasons, are seldom given convincing ones. They are bombarded with hard work, labeled education — not seen therefore as child labor. They rise for school at the same time or earlier than their fathers, start work without office chatter, go till noon without coffee breaks, have waxed milk for lunch instead of dry martinis, then back at the desk till three o'clock. Facing greater threats and riskier decisions than their fathers have had to meet since *their* day in school.

And always at someone else's convenience. Someone else dictates when to rise, what's to be good for breakfast, what's to be learned in school, what's to be good for lunch, what're to be play hours, what're to be homework hours,

what's to be delicious for dinner and what's to be, suddenly, bedtime. This goes on until summer — when there is, once again, a "leisure problem." "What," the child asks, "am I going to do with myself?" Millions of things, as it turns out, but no sooner have they been discovered than it is time to go back to school.

It should come as no surprise, then, that within this shifting hodgepodge of external pressures, a child, simply to save his sanity, must go underground. Have a place to hide where he cannot be got at by grownups. A place that implies, if only obliquely, that *they're* not so much; that *they* don't know everything; that *they* can't fly the way some people can, or let bullets bounce harmlessly off their chests, or beat up whoever picks on them, or — oh, joy of joys ! — even become invisible! A no-man's land. A relief zone. And the basic sustenance for this relief was, in my day, comic books. With them we were able to roam free, disguised in costume, committing the greatest of feats — and the worst of sins. And, in every instance, getting away with them. For a little while, at least, it was our show. For a little while, at least, we were the bosses. Psychically renewed, we could then return above ground and put up with another couple of days of victimization. Comic books were our booze.

Just as in earlier days for other children it was pulps and *Nick Carter* and penny dreadfuls — all junk in their own right, but less disapproved of latterly because they were less

violent. But, predictably, as the ante on violence rose in the culture, so too did it rise in the junk.

3.

Comic books, which had few public (as opposed to professional) defenders in the days when Dr. Wertham was attacking them, are now looked back on by an increasing number of my generation as samples of our youthful innocence instead of our youthful corruption. A sign, perhaps, of the potency of that corruption. A corruption — a lie, really — that put us in charge, however temporarily, of the world in which we lived and gave us the means, however arbitrary, of defining right from wrong, good from bad hero from villain. It is something for which old fans can understandably pine — almost as if having become overly conscious of the imposition of junk on our adult values: on our architecture, our highways, our advertising, our mass media, our politics — and even in the air we breathe, flying black chunks of it — we have staged a retreat to a better remembered brand of junk. A junk that knew its place was underground where it had no power and thus only titillated, rather than above ground where it truly has power — and thus, only depresses. ❖

The Vault of Horror #32, © August 1953 William M. Gaines.

THOUSANDS OF VOLTS SLAMMED THROUGH HER BODY, TEARING AND BURNING...DESTROYING FLESH, BONE, TISSUE! THOUSANDS OF VOLTS PULSATING, COURSING THROUGH EVERY FIBRE OF HER BEING... MAKING HER TORSO SURGE AND STRAIN AT THE STRAPS THAT HELD HER!

BLACKNESS. PAINLESS, TORTURELESS BLACKNESS. THE EMPTINESS BECOMING SOMETHING. SOLIDITY! A FLOOR? YES! SHE WAS LYING ON A FLOOR SOMEWHERE... AND THE EBONY VOID BECAME SOLID WALLS. FOUR SOLID WALLS, A CEILING AND A FLOOR...BUT NO WAY OUT!

ABOUT THE AUTHOR

Jules Feiffer, one of America's most influential editorial cartoonists, is also a playwright, novelist, screenwriter and author of children's books. His trademark visual style typically features sparely drawn, neurotic characters, appearing against blank backgrounds, and emoting or agonizing over news events and personal problems. His weekly strip *Feiffer* appeared in the *Village Voice* from 1956 to 1997, and a retrospective exhibition of his work appeared at the Library of Congress in 1996, and in February 2003 a three month retrospective appeared at the New York Historical Society. His cartoon collections include *Feiffer on Nixon: The Cartoon Presidency* (1974), *Ronald Reagan in Movie America* (1988), and *Feiffer: The Collected Works*, Volumes 1, 2, and 3 (1988, 1989, 1992). *Tantrum* (reissued in 1997) was his comic strip novel. (He rejects the term 'graphic novel.') His first satiric cartoon *Munro* was animated in 1960 and won an Academy Award. In 1986, he won the Pulitzer Prize for editorial cartooning and in 1994 he was elected to the American Academy of Arts and Letters.

Feiffer's work in other genres is characterized by the same talent for social satire and commentary. His 1967 play *Little Murders* is a brutal black comedy that examines one New York City family's encounters with random and senseless violence. The play received a number of prestigious awards, including the London Theatre Critics, Outer Circle Critics and Obie Awards. New York Times theater reviewer Clive Barnes said of *Little Murders*, "[Feiffer] muses on urban man, the cesspool of urban man's mind, the beauty of his neurosis, and the inevitability of his wilting disappointment." *Little Murders* was adapted to film in 1971 starring Elliott Gould and Marcia Rodd. Feiffer's other plays include the Obie-winning *White House Murder Case* (1970), *Knock Knock* (1976), *Elliot Loves* (1989) and his latest, *A Bad Friend* (2003).

Feiffer was born in the Bronx, N.Y., in 1929. At the age of five he won a gold medal in an art contest, a reward gained so effortlessly that it immediately decided him upon a career. After high school, he enrolled at the Art Students League of New York and attended drawing classes at Pratt Institute in Brooklyn.

He sought employment with several comic strip artists, including Will Eisner, creator of *The Spirit*, who allowed Feiffer to write scripts for him until the aspiring cartoonist was drafted into the Army at what he claims was a slight increase in pay. From 1949 to 1951 Feiffer drew a Sunday cartoon-page feature called *Clifford*, which ran in six newspapers. Feiffer then served

a two-year stint in the Signal Corps, which he described as his passive resistance period. He spent his off hours drawing anti-military cartoons and during this time developed the character of Munro, the four-year-old boy drafted by mistake, into the Army.

After he got out of the Army, Feiffer drifted from one job to another, managing not to get fired until he worked the six months required to collect unemployment insurance. During his non-working period he turned out a book of cartoons called *Sick, Sick, Sick*. His *Munro* was turned into an animated feature in 1960. The critic Gilbert Millstein has referred to Feiffer as being "alone and unafraid in a world made of just about all of the intellectual shams and shibboleths to which our culture subscribes."

Feiffer also likes to write occasional novels, publishing his first, *Harry the Rat with Women* in 1963, and his second, *Ackroyd* in 1967. He is also author of the screenplays for *Little Murders, Carnal Knowledge* and *Popeye*.

The Man in the Ceiling was Feiffer's first book for children. Highly praised in *The New York Times* and elsewhere, it was selected by *Publishers Weekly* and The New York Public Library as one of the best children's books of 1993. Since then Feiffer has released *A Barrel of Laughs, A Vale of Tears* (1995), his first all-color picture book, *Meanwhile* (1997), *I Lost My Bear* (1998) *Bark, George!* (1999), *I'm Not Bobby!* (2001), *By The Side of the Road* (2001), and *The House Across the Street* (2002).

In May of 1997, Feiffer left the *Village Voice* following a salary dispute. He was immediately picked up by *The New York Times* as their first monthly op-ed cartoonist. He retired his syndicated strip two years later (1999) to concentrate on children's books, teaching, and his return to theatre. He became a Senior Fellow in the National Arts Journalism Program at Columbia University's Graduate School of Journalism.

Jules Feiffer and his wife Jenny, a writer and stand-up comic, live in New York City and on Martha's Vineyard. He is the father of three daughters and a grandfather.